RUDOLF STEINER (1861–1925) called his spiritual philosophy 'anthroposophy', meaning 'wisdom of the human being'. As a highly developed seer, he based his work on direct knowledge and perception of spiritual dimensions. He initiated a modern and universal 'science of spirit', accessible to anyone willing to exercise clear and unprejudiced thinking.

From his spiritual investigations Steiner provided suggestions for the renewal of many activities, including education (both general and special), agriculture, medicine, economics, architecture, science, philosophy, religion and the arts. Today there are thousands of schools, clinics, farms and other organizations involved in practical work based on his principles. His many published works feature his research into the spiritual nature of the human being, the evolution of the world and humanity, and methods of personal development. Steiner wrote some 30 books and delivered over 6000 lectures across Europe. In 1924 he founded the General Anthroposophical Society, which today has branches throughout the world.

Rudolf Steiner was not concerned with systems. His aim was to suggest impulses towards finding and developing ways of living that would be worthy of humanity in the here and now. One aspect of this was his wish to intensify our awareness of existence as something that is not limited to our present life between birth and death. He never tired of reminding us that we are in reality spiritual entities. Through his written works and lectures Steiner urged us to take this hidden reality seriously, encouraging us in countless ways to develop an awareness of spirituality—a presence of mind that would enable us to recognize and do what is necessary in any given moment. Yet when faced with the voluminous dimensions of his work, it is easy to lose sight of this.

The '**spiritual perspectives**' presented in this series assemble core ideas on specific subjects, as found in his complete works, with the aim of bringing mobility into thinking while also deepening the ability to understand and act. The brief extracts do not claim to provide exhaustive treatment of a subject. Their purpose is to open up approaches to the prodigious complex of Steiner's work, so as to assist readers as they endeavour to gain their own understanding of his extraordinary world of ideas.

The source references are intended to serve as initial signposts. However, some will find the fragments sufficient in themselves—as valuable aids to making one's way in the complex world that surrounds us.

ON FEAR

spiritual perspectives

RUDOLF STEINER

compiled and edited by Taja Gut
translated by J. Collis

RUDOLF STEINER PRESS

Rudolf Steiner Press
Hillside House, The Square
Forest Row, RH18 5ES

www.rudolfsteinerpress.com

Published by Rudolf Steiner Press 2011

Originally published in German under the title *Stichwort Angst* by Rudolf Steiner Verlag, Dornach, in 2010. This authorized translation is published by permission of the Rudolf Steiner Nachlassverwaltung, Dornach

A catalogue record for this book is available from the British Library

ISBN: 978 1 85584 263 2

Cover by Andrew Morgan Design
Typeset by DP Photosetting, Neath, West Glamorgan
Printed and bound by Gutenberg Press, Malta

MIX
Paper from
responsible sources
FSC
www.fsc.org FSC® C022612

CONTENTS

1. FEAR AND ITS EFFECTS

Fearlessness ensures against loss of soul strength

One could say that human beings have more feelings than those which the physical world alone induces in them. In ordinary life this excess is employed in a certain way, namely in a way that must be transformed into something else by esoteric schooling.* Take, for example, a feeling of anxiety or fear. It is easy to see that in many cases the fear or anxiety is greater than would be appropriate for a particular happening. Now imagine the esoteric pupil working energetically on himself to ensure that in any instance he feels only the amount of fear or anxiety that is truly appropriate for the external process in question. Well, any application of soul forces always generates a certain measure of fear or anxiety. This amount of soul force is indeed lost through the production of fear or anxiety. So the esoteric pupil saves this soul force by denying himself the fear or the anxiety, as well as other things. So it then remains at his disposal for something else. When this procedure is repeated frequently, the soul forces thus continuously saved form an inner store so that the pupil soon begins to experience how, out of such saved up portions of feeling, inner pictures begin to germinate which express revelations of the life in higher realms.[1]

---

* Esoteric or spiritual science will create certainty about the greatest riddles of existence. It is called esoteric science not because it conceals something but because its teachings must be found in one's innermost being. It is esoteric in the same way that mathematics is an esoteric science.[2]

Dangers and reality of fear in the spiritual world

Human beings are surrounded by spiritual worlds which are to the ordinary sphere of the senses as is the world of colour, radiance and light to a blind person's sphere of touch ... These worlds of the spirit surround us on all sides. But as well as being worlds of paradise and blessedness—although they do have paradise and blessedness within them—they are also worlds that can be fearful for us, dangerous on account of certain facts and also beings. If we wish to gain knowledge of the loftiness and blessedness contained in these worlds we can only do so if we also come to know the danger and frightfulness that are in them. The one is not possible without the other.

So we must be clear as to the extent of the danger inherent in this. Imagine someone who without knowing it is standing beside a gunpowder magazine. Then, on suddenly being made aware of his location, he is filled with fright at the idea of being blown to smithereens should the magazine explode. Outwardly nothing has changed and yet for him life has changed utterly. The one thing that is different is the fact that he is now aware of the danger. This knowledge distinguishes him from those who do not possess this knowledge.

The situation as regards the higher worlds is the same. The danger and frightfulness contained in them is always around us. Indeed, huge dangers for our soul lurk in worlds about which we possess not the slightest inkling. With regard to these dangers and this frightfulness the only difference between those who have never approached spiritual science and those who have made contact with it is that the latter know about the dangers while the former do not.

And yet perhaps this is not entirely so, for the following reason: We step into the spiritual world where that which is spiritual is at work. The gunpowder magazine does not become dangerous because you are afraid that the powder might explode. But your fear is something that has meaning in the spiritual world! There is a difference between your having this fear or not having it because the thoughts you cultivate introduce something real into the spiritual world. The feeling of hatred with which you approach someone is much more real in the spiritual world and also much more effective for the one who is aware of it than is a blow with a stick administered to the object of your hatred.[3]

Fear is suppressed hatred

There are two things which we should endeavour to avoid entirely during our esoteric schooling. We should never injure another individual, either through something we do or in what we think and say; neither should we put forward the excuse that it was not our intention to injure anyone. There is no difference between doing it on purpose or by accident.

The other thing to avoid is the feeling of hatred; this must be banned entirely from our feelings, otherwise it will reappear as a feeling of fear. Fear is suppressed hatred! Hatred must be transformed into a feeling of love, namely of love for wisdom.[4]

Feelings of fear nourish inimical spiritual powers

Fear and anxiety, negative feelings like this, can indeed become disastrous when they emanate from human beings who are getting to know spiritual beings and forces. Anxiety and fear bring us into a disastrous relationship with the spiritual world. The reason for this is that in the spiritual world there are beings who find welcome nourishment in the fear and anxiety emanating from us. Such beings starve when there is no fear or anxiety coming to them from humanity. Those of us who are not yet thoroughly familiar with the matter might take this statement as an analogy. But those who understand the situation know very well that it expresses a reality. When we send forth fear and anxiety and panic, this provides welcome nourishment for those beings, and they grow to be more and more powerful. They are inimical to us. All beings who are nourished by negative feelings, by anxiety, fear and superstition, by hopelessness and doubt are in the spiritual world inimical to humanity; they launch vicious attacks on us when they receive nourishment from those feelings. It is therefore essential above all that when we enter into the spiritual world we should first arm ourselves against fear, hopelessness, doubt and anxiety.[5]

The power of unconscious fear

In western civilization the human being acts as a cloak which is covering a focal point of destruction, and the forces of decline can only be transformed into the forces of ascent once people become aware that they do indeed provide a cloak for a focal point of destruction.

What would happen if spiritual science did not make us aware of this? Well, in the way times are developing today we can already see what would happen. Something that is to a certain extent isolated, set apart within the human being and which ought to be working solely within him while occupying the one location where matter is thrown back into chaos, that something is forcing its way out; it is entering into external human instincts. This is what will become western civilization and thus earth civilization. This is revealing itself in all the destructive forces now appearing for example in the eastern part of Europe.* It is the destructive fury which is being thrown into the outer world from within the human being. Not until we have once more attained genuine knowledge about the human being and thus become aware of that human focal point of destruction shall we be able in future to find our way about in all that is spilling over into our instincts. That focal point of destruction has to be present inside us for the sake of the development of our capacity to think, for it is strength in thinking that we need in order to gain a view of the world which is appropriate for today. This strength in thinking must exist before the mirror of our memory. There it will bring about the continuation of thinking in the ether body; and this ether body permeated by thinking will have a destructive effect on the physical body. It is a fact that this focal point of destruction is present in modern western human beings. What the knowledge does is to draw our attention to this fact ...

It was initially fear that overcame the pupils in the esoteric colonies about which I have spoken when they first heard about these mysteries. They became very thoroughly acquainted with fear. They became thoroughly acquainted

---

* Reference to the Russian civil war of 1918–21 (Ed.)

with the sense that the act of looking into the inner being of man—not dishonestly, as in a form of nebulous mysticism, but honestly—must generate fear. In the old esoteric schools of the West this fear could only be banished by teaching the pupils to be aware of the entire import of the facts. Then, through consciousness, they were able to conquer the fear that could not but be generated.

Then, when the age of intellectualism began, this fear became unconscious, and as such it continues to work today. It appears in our external life in all kinds of disguises. For modern times it became appropriate to look into the inner being of man. 'Know yourself!' became a legitimate challenge. Indeed, by the very generation of fear which could then be conquered the esoteric pupils were made aware of self-knowledge in the right way. The age of intellectualism dulled the ability to look into man's inner being; but it could not banish fear entirely. And thus it came about that people were and remained under the impression of this unconscious fear to the degree that they said and say: 'There is absolutely nothing in the human being that reaches beyond birth and death.' They are afraid of looking beyond the life of memory, beyond this ordinary life of thought which is governed only by the laws that apply between birth and death. They are afraid to look deeply into what is genuinely eternal in the human soul. And it is by this fear that they justify the doctrine: 'There is absolutely nothing but this life between birth and death.'

Modern materialism has arisen out of fear, without people having the slightest inkling about this. The modern materialistic world view is a product of fear and anxiety.[6]

Feelings of fear and the beings of evil

We know that the stream of humanity is already in the process of dividing into two parts, the one which goes towards the virtuous and the moral, and the other which culminates in what is gruesome and evil. These conditions are already in the making; the seeds for them are already germinating. Thus all the machines and gadgets now in existence which can be set in motion will become frightful, horrible demons on Jupiter.* All the things which serve only the principle of usefulness will some day become strong and frightful forces of this kind. This process can be halted if we transform the equipment which serves only usefulness into objects which, as well as being useful, also proclaim, above all, their beauty, that which is godlike. It is a very good thing that we know this. Otherwise forces of this kind would one day tear the earth to pieces. We see, too, that we should surround the upbringing and education of our children with artistic impressions. Art makes us free. Even a railway locomotive must one day be transformed into a machine that is beautiful.

Our feelings of fear and anxiety are nourishment for other evil beings. We must not permit such thoughts to arise, for on Jupiter demons like this will surround us in far greater numbers than is the case today. But there will be nothing of this kind to fear for those who are prudent enough to keep their surroundings pure, so that no flies can gather amongst the dirt.[7]

---

*Steiner's term for a future incarnation of the earth. (Ed.)

Fear of the spiritual world

There is present in the soul not only what we know in the ordinary way, for things happen in the depths of our soul experience that cast their shadow, or their light, up into ordinary consciousness. But our ordinary consciousness does not reach down to these things. Hidden in the depths of our soul there may be hatred and love, joy and fear and excitement without any of these feelings being present in the part of our soul life that is conscious. So it is perfectly possible for a particular manifestation of conscious hatred from one person to another to be the result of a love that has roots deep within the soul. In the depths of a person's soul there may be profound sympathy for another person. But because the person also has reasons, perhaps equally unknown to him, he might stifle this love, or this sympathy, and delude himself that what he feels is hatred and antipathy.

This is something that holds sway in the hidden depths of our soul, so in these depths things can look utterly different from what is found in our upper consciousness. Conditions of fear and anxiety may exist in the depths of the soul without the person in question knowing anything about it in his ordinary upper consciousness. Because there is an abyss that must be traversed before one can enter into the spiritual world, someone might have in the depths of his soul a fear and an anxiety about that world without noticing any such thing in the upper part of his consciousness. In fact all those who have not yet entered the spiritual world but who have attained a certain amount of knowledge about it have in some degree this horror, this fear of the spiritual world. Whatever we might think about this fear and this anxiety which lie deep within the soul, they merely appear more strongly in some and less strongly in others. And because the soul might be harmed in some way a wise arrangement of our being sees to it that we cannot easily look into the spiritual world, for we must first experience the Guardian of the Threshold when we are ready. Until this happens we remain protected.[8]

Fear and idleness are related

Fear is related to idleness, to the wish to cling to habits. Why are people afraid of changing their situation? Because they are idle! This idleness is related to fear. Earlier we described what can sometimes be the basis for hatred. Well, one can also say that fear is related to indolence or idleness.[9]

Fear of the supposedly unknown

Human beings always feel odd when faced with the unknown; and the feeling they have over against the unknown is, above all, one of fear. Compared with everything we can experience in the world of the senses, what we meet when researching the spiritual world is something unknown, and the difficulties are the same when we want to speak about that world. We are afraid of the spiritual world, but the fear we have is an unusual one because it is a fear of which we are unaware. How does the materialistic, the mechanistic ... view of the world come about? It comes about because in our soul we are afraid to break out of the sense-perceptible world; we are afraid of breaking away from sensory things and arriving in the unknown, in nothingness, as Mephistopheles says to Faust. And Faust replies: 'It is my hope that in your nothingness I shall find the All.' It is a fear of something that one senses must be nothingness, but it is a fear in disguise, a fear that wears a mask! We must realize that soul processes exist which are subconscious or even unconscious, soul processes which expand in rank profusion in the depths of our soul life. It is worth noting that people deceive themselves about a good many things. For example, one delusion that occurs very frequently is that when people want something for utterly egoistic reasons they do not admit to themselves that egoism is the reason. Instead they invent all kinds of excuses, saying that they want to do something for quite selfless reasons or out of charity. By saying this they hide their egoism under a mask. This happens very often in fraternities which come together in order, for example, to do charitable works out of love ...

Today it is fear which leads to the rejection of spiritual science. But it is a fear to which people do not admit. It is in their souls, but they do not allow it to come up into consciousness. Instead they invent proofs with which to oppose spiritual science, proofs which warn against the danger of entering into the realm of fantasy when one leaves the firm ground of sensory perception, and so on. People do indeed invent extremely complicated proofs. They construct entire philosophies which can often not be disproved by logic ... Yet these are actually nothing other than a fear of allowing one's soul to set out along a path that will lead to a concrete experience of something which one feels is unknown. These are the two main reasons behind the lack of understanding for spiritual science: a weakness of our life of soul, and fear of something that is supposedly unknown.[10]

Physical matter as an ahrimanic illusion generates fear

At night the luciferic beings influence us as though from the inside, while during the day the ahrimanic-mephistophelian beings do the same from the outside. So what have these beings achieved within us by means of their influence? Together with freedom and 'I'-consciousness, the luciferic beings have given us the most extreme expression of the latter, namely *hatred*. Human beings would never have been capable of hatred if they had not increasingly secluded themselves within their own 'I'. And the ahrimanic beings enveloped the divine, spiritual world in the fog of maya or illusion, thus hiding it from human eyes, so that we are no longer able to see what lies behind physical things. It is because of this that *fear* has arisen. We would never have known fear if we had been able to see the divine creators instead of bumping into physical objects in space. Small children learn to have fear as soon as they come into contact with matter by bumping into it.

In order to make progress, the esoteric pupil must now endeavour to divest himself of these two, of hatred and fear, even in all their most subtle manifestations.[11]

Fear makes us susceptible to black magic

The first requirement is to go beyond whatever connects us with only one portion of humanity. This is the first principle for a white magician today. It is not selflessness for which a person can strive, but love for all humanity. He can broaden the range of his love. This is what he can do, and it is with this that we are concerned here ...

You see, someone wanting to become a black magician nowadays would already possess a huge stock of what he needed for the workings of his black magic if he were a terrible coward who was horribly frightened of everything that might happen to him. To have such fear within himself would be a very good starting point for the black magician, for fear is nothing other than compressed egoism. Let us suppose that someone were intending to practise the arts of black magic on a largish scale. He would begin by looking around for individuals who were as cowardly as possible. This stock of fear is a useful medium because it can be remoulded and transformed in such a way that the chicken-hearted individuals in question would gain certain other forces and powers, without any knowledge or insight, on a much larger scale than is normal for human beings. What would a magician like this have to do in order to develop skills of this kind? The first thing would be to set up a laboratory in which to train those chicken-hearted individuals—I am speaking radically, but this will make the matter all the clearer for you—to harden themselves by again and again cutting into living flesh and watching the blood run out. In the feelings of fear, which a chicken-hearted person has in a high degree, a certain force is at work outwardly which can be transformed into its opposite when individuals are taught to inure themselves by cutting into living flesh.

Such a procedure would be entirely pointless in the case of an individual who had no fear.

This, then, is what you might describe as the very first step to be taken in black magic. When this is done, the fear that is present in the individual is transformed into powers by means of which he can indeed exercise a certain influence over his environment. So someone making use of minions like this would be able to inflict unbelievably horrible atrocities upon the world ...

If you think seriously about this matter, you might ask yourself what could perhaps protect most people against procedures of the kind just described, by means of which individuals could most certainly be led towards gaining command of the powers of black magic. Egoism is very good as a protection against such things. Not everyone will have the stomach to cut into living flesh; most people are likely to fall down in a faint, and this kind of unconsciousness is nothing other than an expression of selfishness. Such a physical effect is therefore a good way of being prevented from practising black magic.[12]

Animals live in a world of fear

Are people today still capable of seeing in many animals the anxious, fearful glance with which whole groups of them look out into the world? We shall indeed one day learn to see it again when the capacity for abstraction has reached the point of driving us to the Guardian of the Threshold, for then we may once again develop sympathy with the animals! I do not mean the kind of sympathy which we are often artificially taught to feel, but a sympathy which is akin to an elemental inner experience. It can be said that a specific kind of fearfulness, an anxious way of looking out into the world, is prevalent among all the higher, the warm-blooded animals. . . .

Fearfulness is a general characteristic of animals. Those

that are not afraid have been trained in some way. Fearfulness is intrinsic in animals because they possess in a high degree the capacity for abstraction, for abstract concepts. Animals live in these abstractions. The world with which you become familiar after prolonged studying, after dealing in abstractions for a long time, is the world in which the animals are at home. Meanwhile the world in which human beings live through their senses here on earth is much less familiar to animals despite the fact that they, too, possess senses.

It is profoundly true that what one does not know makes one afraid. Animals look out upon the world with fearfulness. Something which I mentioned the other day is rather important, and this is that human beings are afraid of the life of the spirit. How can it be that they are so afraid? It has come about because they now have to approach the Guardian of the Threshold in their subconsciousness. There they stand, faced with this decision about which I have spoken. And in this they come to be more like the animals. Animals are fearful. They are passing through the realm of fear. That is how these things are connected. And this state of being fearful will increase greatly if human beings do not make earnest endeavours to become properly acquainted with and take into themselves that world, the spiritual world, which must come towards them.[13]

Fearfulness while sleeping

When we go further in our sleep we enter into other stages that can no longer be comprehended by means of imaginative knowledge. To comprehend these we need inspired knowledge. Once again we meet with facts of soul experience. In inspired consciousness these are mirrored in the same way as the pulsation of the blood is mirrored in joy and sorrow. In a certain way the soul is here distributed among as many separate spiritual beings as possible. The life of the soul is actually split up into parts and this splitting up is connected with something which appears as fearfulness when it shines up into consciousness ... It is necessary for human beings to transcend this fearfulness.[14]

Anxiety and egoism

On the path of initiation there exists a mysterious connection between on the one hand everything that the human being can bring about out of his egoism and, on the other hand, all that can be expressed by the word 'anxiety'. Once a person has reached the stage of being able to look into the spiritual world without any egoism he will have no more anxiety. Anxiety is a concomitant of egoism. Even if you cannot believe that while anxiety is still present egoism cannot yet have disappeared, nevertheless the fact is that on the long journey into the spiritual world, which demands so much by way of renunciation, egoism must disappear without trace. If someone enters the spiritual world while there is still some egoism left in him, then anxiety will come and show itself with all its destructive might.

In this we see something of the dangers that are involved in initiation. In the sense-perceptible world the benevolent powers of the spiritual realm make sure that anxiety cannot approach human beings in that way. But as soon as they unite with the spiritual world and meet the powers at work there, forces like anxiety turn into destructive powers. One can overcome all sorts of things by using the keys which lead the way into the spiritual world; but anxiety creeps in through every keyhole. However, once the individual has progressed far enough, then, if he confronts it courageously, anxiety becomes a force which relieves him of even that very last vestige of egoism . . .[15]

Pathological fear

A series of newspaper articles on arteriosclerosis described the concomitant symptoms which enable people to observe this disease in themselves. The author of a pamphlet about this, a medical doctor, then noticed quite a number of patients coming to consult him because they imagined they had the symptoms of arteriosclerosis. We may conclude from this that owing to the chaotic nature of our culture the state of mind of very many people . . . is such that they only have to hear about a disease of this kind in order to be influenced to the extent that they do indeed become ill, though only in a psychological form. It is said that frequently people only have to attend lectures by Professor So-and-so or nature-cure practitioner Mr So-and-so in order to find themselves suffering from the very diseases described. What is not taken into account, however, is that you have to be suffering from a specific form of psychological illness in order to think in this way in the first place! This is a pathological trait which is relatively harmless today but which will in the future become increasingly damaging . . .

The foundation upon which human beings base their convictions must always be derived from what is within them. For this to be possible their mind and spirit must be stronger.

They must be capable of discovering their convictions within themselves. It is feebleness of mind and spirit that prevents them from believing in themselves and from believing that they can find the reasons for certainty within themselves. It is feebleness of mind and spirit to believe only in what their eyes can see and their hands can touch and to want to take hold of the truth with their hands alone. Materialism is a sign of spiritual and mental decadence, an emptiness of mind. If it were merely a theoretical emptiness it would be relatively harmless. But this theoretical emptiness leads to a practical undermining first of one's psychological and then of one's physical health. The truth about the example quoted is that sick and erroneous thoughts bring about actual illnesses.[16]

2. DEATH, FEAR OF DEATH AND FEAR OF THE UNKNOWN

The Guardian of the Threshold

The moment we step outside ourselves clairvoyantly in everyday life we see the Guardian of the Threshold. He shields us from an experience which we must first learn how to endure. First of all we must have within ourselves the strength which enables us to say: 'Before us lies a future world, and we look without any terror or dread upon what we have become, for we know with utter certainty that we are capable of making amends for all of it.' It is during the period of preparation for clairvoyant research that we must acquire the capacity to experience this moment without being depressed by it. This preparation—let us again speak in the abstract, for we shall be dealing with the concrete situation later on—calls upon us to make the active and positive aspects of our soul as strong and as energetic as we possibly can and to increase in the utmost degree our courage, our sense of freedom, our love, our energy for thinking, and our energy for clear-sighted intellectual thought, so that we may step outside our physical body not as weaklings but as strong individuals. If we have in us too much of what in ordinary life we are familiar with as anxiety and fear we shall not be able to endure this experience without being cast down by it. [17]

Spiritual science gives us strength for our encounter with the Guardian of the Threshold

First of all we have to become thoroughly familiar with spiritual science. When we do this, the grand, the all-embracing, the strengthening and encouraging and refreshing ideas and thoughts of this science give our soul not only mere theory, but also characteristics of feeling, will and thinking as the result of which it is able to become as strong as steel. After preparations of this kind the moment of encountering the Guardian of the Threshold will be something other than it would be without such preparation. If the encounter is preceded by learning about the higher worlds, any conditions of fear and apprehension will be overcome in an entirely different manner than would otherwise be the case.[18]

A trial of the soul: Boundless fear of emptiness

And then, when the soul feels that with today's normal consciousness it can bring forth nothing but ideas which are maya in comparison with full-blooded reality, when the soul is not a lemon squeezed dry as a result of recognizing only the sciences of today, then it feels empty in the face of universal reality. Although it feels able to reach out with its ideas to the ends of the world, to the far distances of the universe, nevertheless it is not taking into account the statement heard in the second Mystery Drama *The Soul's Probation*: 'End not in the far distances of the universe.' A person seriously wanting to stop upon reaching the far distances of the universe would be unable to avoid being assailed by the feeling of having to spread himself across endless space with ideas which as such are anyway feeble. There they would become even more attenuated, and the more we travel towards the far distances of the universe the thinner still they become until we find ourselves on the brink of the endlessly empty abyss with our ideas. This has to occur as a trial of the soul. A person thirsting for reality who has to solve the riddles and the wonders of the world in accordance with the abstract sciences will ultimately find himself faced with universal emptiness as his ideas evaporate entirely in a spiritual haze. When this happens the soul cannot but feel an endless fear of emptiness. Those who are unable to feel this fear of emptiness are quite simply not yet advanced enough to be able to sense the truth about present-day consciousness.

So if we want to expand present-day consciousness out into the far distances of the universe we will be faced with fear of universal emptiness as a terrifying spectre. No one who takes seriously what today's normal consciousness is like can be spared this. It is a trial in which the soul must participate if it wants to experience the meaning and the spirit of our time. Standing at the abyss which opens up on all sides when we endeavour to fathom the distances of space with our present-day ideas, the soul cannot avoid experiencing this endless fear of emptiness, this fear of losing oneself in the universal widths of space. Knowing the world view of Goethe and what he said about becoming one with the universe and expanding oneself to actually become a universe, we have to say: 'If we want to go into the far distances of the universe with the means of knowledge available to us today and if we endeavour to grasp the world with today's philosophical principles, which cannot but be abstract because they derive from present-day consciousness, then a healthy soul will have to go through the trial of standing before emptiness, before the abyss stretching out on all sides, the trial of facing the prospect of being consumed in endless nothingness with the best part of one's being, namely with one's consciousness.'

This is the overall feeling while all the other feelings that are generated by trials of the soul are specialized portions of this fear of emptiness, this *horror vacui*. With our narrowly defined life of soul it would be unhealthy not to sense how present-day consciousness must of necessity explode and splinter into pieces if faced with the endless distances of space in an endeavour to expand and encompass them. This is the fate of the soul if it wants to press forward into the far distances of the universe, into the wide widths of the world with present-day consciousness.[19]

Fear and initiation

Nowadays it can happen that people would like to go through an initiation as if it were something that 'one does' during the course of a lifetime, whenever it happens to be convenient. They want to inform themselves—as we say today—about what it is that leads to the knowledge one gains. But they do not want to experience what people of old had to experience when seeking initiation. They have no wish to be taken hold of in a process involving the whole of their being from preparation right up to illumination, a process that will make a new person of them.

The fact is, however, that they would indeed have to decide to become a new person. The descriptions you often find regarding the ancient mystery cults provide only an unclear idea, for these descriptions, too, make it seem as though the ancient initiations were undertaken in passing, as it were, something like today's so-called initiation into modern Freemasonry ... However, there was in ancient times an essential preparation which had to be undertaken.

A pupil seeking initiation had to go through an inner state of soul, which can only be described by saying that he had to be guided in the strongest degree through the fear which a human being always feels when he is being led truthfully and genuinely in full consciousness to face something that is entirely unknown to him. The essential aspect of those ancient initiations was that the pupil had to take into himself with the utmost intensity the feeling that he was about to face something which it would be impossible to face in any way in ordinary external life ... A region of his soul was brought to life in the pupil who was about to undergo initiation, a region which the ordinary person of today and also the ordinary, profane person of olden times avoided within himself, a region he did not want to approach and about which he preferred to harbour illusions. This is described externally—although it must be comprehended rather more inwardly—as the incitement of various conditions of fear. It was necessary for these conditions to be experienced because only that aspect of the soul which is situated in a region that the human being fears in ordinary external life can be guided towards the intended knowledge.

This mood of soul had to be bravely suffered through, and was indeed then experienced. In it the pupil felt nothing but fear of something or other, something unknown, for it was through the fear that he was to be led towards the knowledge. And it was out of this mood of soul that he was guided towards what I just now described as the descent through the regions of heaven or of the spiritual world out of which he was then led upwards again in eight steps, which today can of course only be imitated in accordance with the customs of our time. In those ancient times the pupil was indeed led into this experience.[20]

No fear of the abyss of individuality

We should not wish to renounce the drama of knowledge in favour of a grammar of knowledge. And fear, too, must not be permitted to prevent us from tumbling into the abyss of individuality, for we climb up out of this abyss again in the company of many spirits and experience ourselves as being related to them; it is through this that we are born out of the spiritual world. But we have taken death into ourselves, and we ourselves become destroyers of that which has come into being; we live in its spiritualized form and are present at its destruction.[21]

Existing in nothingness

So long as we feel comfortable in the thoughts, so long as we feel strong in the thoughts, we cannot rise up into the supersensible world. When we follow the thoughts, however, we sense something that contains a double comparison, as though the ground were being removed from under our feet and we were floating in emptiness, or as though we were seeing spread out above us the blue dome of heaven before coming to realize 'The blue dome of heaven is not a blue dome of heaven, for it is I myself—because my ability to see does not reach far enough—who am surrounding the universe with a blue dome of heaven; yet in truth it stretches into the infinite, so that I must truly ask: Where is there a fixed point?' . . .

What I have been telling you is not something constructed out of fantasy, nor is it conceived out of thoughts: it is what everyone experiences who has sought to find the path into the supersensible world. This becomes an experience such as that described in *How to Know Higher Worlds*. What I have thus described as a sensation increases in a certain way in someone who is truly following the path of knowledge until it becomes a feeling which is similar to what we know as fear in our everyday life, a feeling of insecurity that could be described as not knowing where one is standing, not knowing where one is flying, or simply not knowing where one is. However, this feeling must not be permitted to develop fully, it must remain in the subconscious part of the soul because only then can we enter into the supersensible world. This feeling must immediately be illuminated by something which can be compared with a feeling of courage, of energy and the development of the will. We must become aware of something in us which through self-education we can train in slow, patient progress if we frequently have the idea: You not only do or plan to do what external requirements expect of you, what one demand or another requires of you; instead you set yourself the ideal of doing whatever it is out of your own thoughts without losing the will to carry on with it.[22]

Anxiety about falling to pieces in sleep

When we enter into sleep with our soul, the first state we go through—all of this takes place in the unconscious but it is nonetheless vividly encountered—is one in which we feel ourselves to be living within a universal world of the etheric. Although I say 'feel' I mean an unconscious feeling; one can only describe these things with the help of expressions that are familiar to us in our ordinary consciousness. We feel as though we were spread out across the whole cosmos. The concrete view to which we are accustomed—our links with the objects that are all around us in our earthly environment—this specific concrete view ceases. Initially we begin to share in a general way in the living and weaving of the cosmos. This is connected with the feeling that in our soul we have no ground under our feet. This experience of having no ground to stand on leads in our soul to a strong desire to be divinely supported. Every day as we fall asleep we experience the religious desire for the world to be permeated with something divinely spiritual which spreads out all around us. This is what we experience as we fall asleep. And because of our whole standing within humanity we bring with us into our waking state this need for the divine. We owe this daily revival of our religious need to the experience of sleep ...

As we sleep—remember, this remains unconscious initially although it is no less vividly experienced—something else comes about; it is as though we are no longer spread all around the cosmos in our soul but are instead divided up among the separate parts of our own being. We feel we are falling to pieces, or rather we would feel we were falling to pieces if we were experiencing this consciously. So in the depths of our soul an unconscious fearfulness begins to assert itself. We experience this fearfulness about being spread out all over the universe every night while we are asleep ...

And this fearfulness, which arises quite soon after we fall asleep, can only be remedied by having a truly strong relationship with the Christ.[23]

Development entails a desire for death

Thus we see that at birth the human being wakes up from the spiritual world in such a way that he now brings with him forces which differ from those which he brings from that same spiritual world on waking up in the morning. In the morning we only bring with us those forces which are able to develop our life of soul during the period between birth and death. Here we are not able to have an effect on the other members of our being. When we enter into existence from the spiritual world at birth, however, we bring those forces with us that mould and transform our physical body and our ether body, in other words forces that bring about development which includes that of the physical and the ether body.

If we were unable to destroy our physical and ether body, if the physical body were unable to go through death, then it would not be possible for us to include our experiences in our development. This is the point at which we have to realize that however much we look towards death with fear and dread and however much we approach our own death with suffering and pain, if we look at the world from a point of view that lies above the personal we have to say: 'It is essential for us to desire death! For death alone enables us to destroy this physical body in order that we may build up a new one in our next life so as to bring all our earthly fruits into life.'[24]

Looking death in the face

At the moment when we perceive the portal through which we pass at our death we also see very many forces that hinder us or even approach us destructively. In most cases, however, it is we who attract these forces towards us because of our fear of death. The greater our fear of death, the greater is their power. The fear of death is one part of fearful feelings in general. Those forces and powers look like shrivelled up sacks when we make ourselves strong in knowing that no fear of death whatsoever can change anything to do with the event of death.

We can only overcome our fear of death and learn to look it courageously in the face if we know that an immortal, eternal core resides within us for which death is no more than a transformation of life, a change in the form life takes. Once we find that immortal core within us through spiritual science we can increasingly train ourselves to overcome such feelings until we also finally overcome what we call the fear of death. The more materialistic we become, on the other hand, the more do we fear death. No science of the spirit can protect us against seeing the truth of what lies behind the scenes. Spiritual science must show us how eternal life, how karma brings with it a great balancing-out in spiritual life. Spiritual science must show us all manner of things. It cannot show us the blessedness that lies behind the scenes of external life without at the same time showing us the terrible forces, the enemies, which lurk in the background. This is unquestionably true, but it also shows us how we can overcome all fear of these adversaries. It shows us how we can confront all such things with a free and courageous vision. If we relinquish ourselves patiently to its teachings, it shows us how to become objective and unprejudiced.[25]

Fear of death: fear of a change in consciousness

There is no such thing as death in the spiritual world but only a change of consciousness. The greatest fear that human beings have, which is the fear of death, cannot be felt by someone for whom the supersensible world has risen up after death. At the moment of passing through the portal of death a person's condition becomes one of intense sensitivity, but he can only exist in a state of consciousness that is either clear or darkened, and it would be quite extraordinary to imagine that a person could be dead in the supersensible world.

There is no such thing as death for the beings who belong to the higher hierarchies except for one exception, the Christ. But for a supersensible being such as the Christ to pass through death he first had to descend to the earth. What is so immeasurably important about the Mystery of Golgotha is the fact that a Being who would never have been able to experience death in His own realm in the sphere of the will had to descend to the earth in order to experience something that is peculiar to human beings, namely death. That inner bond, that profound inner bond between humanity on earth and the Christ was forged when that Being passed through death in order to share this destiny with humanity. That death, as I have already pointed out, is of the utmost importance chiefly for our current earthly evolution.[26]

3. FEAR OF THE FUTURE AND TRUST IN DESTINY

Composure in facing the future

We must eradicate root and branch any fear and dread in our soul concerning the future that is coming towards us. How full of fear and alarm people are today in facing anything that lies in the future, but especially in facing the hour of their own death! We must develop composure with regard to all the feelings and sensations we have about the future; we must anticipate with absolute equanimity whatever may be coming towards us, thinking only that whatever it may be will be brought to us by the wisdom-filled guidance of the universe. Over and over again we must place this before our soul. This will lead to our being able to receive like a gift the powers that allow us to look back into past lives on the earth.[27]

Fighting against destiny saps the will

Composure makes us stronger, never weaker, with regard to life. Anger and impatience make us weak. Composure makes us strong enough to cope with any event. But our will grows ever weaker and weaker if we complain and fight against destiny in an unnatural way.[28]

Fear of a new life

What happens is that before entering the physical world through conception and birth, while still in the spiritual world, we go through an important event which sends out rays into our coming new life. Here on earth we die and pass through the portal of death, we lay aside our physical body and take our soul into the spiritual world. This soul still carries with it the effects of everything it has experienced here in the physical world. Basically, having passed through the portal of death, the soul actually looks just like the effects of what it has undergone here on earth. Once they have passed through the portal of death, the souls come face to face with those who are preparing to descend into physical bodies in the near future. (All I can do is tell you about this event, this fact, because these things can only be gleaned from the spiritual world through experience.) The encounter between the souls who have recently passed through the portal of death and those who will soon be passing through the portal of birth into the physical world is an important event. There is something decisive about it. Its purpose to some degree is to inoculate the descending souls with some idea as to what they will find when they arrive here.

It is this encounter that gives children the strangely melancholic stamp they bear when they are born into the world today. They do not want to enter the world about which they learn through this encounter because they then know in some measure how their 'spiritual plumage' will be ruffled by what human beings on earth today are steeped in on account of the materialistic outlook, the materialistic world view and also materialistic actions. This event, which of course can only be confirmed in spirit, starkly illumines the whole of present-day life which we can and also should learn to comprehend on the basis of a background such as this.[29]

A prenatal feeling of fear of the infinite leads to a new incarnation

Before conception we live within the totality of the cosmos which surrounds us. But what lives in our thoughts during our life on earth is a shadow-image within a small space, within the human physical organism, of all that is actually cosmically alive prior to conception.

This is how we may describe one element of the soul's life before birth or before conception. That which we have by way of our thought-life on earth is actually that which is spiritual in the human being in the world outside the earth; it is what we find as the content of his soul before he descends into the physical world. The other element of the soul's life before birth can only be described in the concepts of earthly life as fear. There is something which entirely fills the soul as fear in the period that precedes physical life on earth. But when you hear such a thing you must remember that, as an experience outside the physical body, fear is entirely different from the fear within the body.

Before descending to earth, man is a being of spirit and soul filled with an element of feeling that can only be compared with what he experiences as fear during his life on earth. This fear is well justified for the period of human life about which we are speaking. During the period between death and a new birth, human beings have all kinds of experiences which are possible while they are cosmically bound up with the universe. But towards the end of their time between death and a new birth they as it were grow weary of the cosmic life just as at the end of a life on earth the desiccation and weaknesses of the physical organization makes them grow weary of life on earth. So human beings tire of extraterrestrial life, and this tiredness expresses itself not so much as weariness but rather as fear of the cosmos. So they flee from the cosmos. They sense that the fundamental characteristic of the cosmos is now something which has become foreign to them and which no longer has anything to offer them. They feel a kind of timidity, which is akin to fear, in the face of the element which surrounds them. They want to extricate themselves from the feeling of vastness and concentrate their being within a human physical body.

What the earth now holds out towards an individual is something like a force of attraction for this state of fear in which he finds himself as he once again approaches existence on the earth. If I were to draw a diagram it would be something like this. Imagine the top of the skull with the brain inside it . . . Well, the forms of the brain with their remarkable convolutions represent, as I have frequently pointed out, a kind of copy of the starry heavens, of the universe. The starry heavens are indeed copied in those cellular tissues of the brain. While living in the cosmos, in the world of the stars, before coming down into the earthly realm, the individual did indeed embrace the starry universe in his whole spiritual being. But now he is afraid of it. He gathers himself together in order to fit into the human brain, that earthly copy of the starry heavens.

This now brings us to what we might call the choice which soul and spirit have to make. The soul makes its way towards that brain which, in the process of being formed, most resembles the starry constellation in which it, the soul, found itself before beginning to descend earthwards . . .

It is essentially the feeling of a kind of fear which leads the soul down into the human realm, a feeling of fear towards the infinite, you might say. This feeling of fear is more to do with the soul aspect. And the world of thought which gradually develops from childhood to adulthood is more the spiritual aspect . . .

It is quite possible to say that the human being as he is in the spiritual and soul world before conception dies upon making the transition towards the physical body. Birth in the physical body represents a death for the spirit and soul of the human being. And when a death occurs a corpse always remains. Just as a corpse remains behind when the human being dies on earth, so does a corpse also remain behind when his aspect of spirit and soul goes towards the earth as the result of conception or—if I may put it like this—when he dies in the heavenly realm. And it is upon this corpse that we draw in our thought-life during the entire course of our time on earth. The corpse is the world of thought; this shadowy world is that which is dead. So when the spiritual aspect of the human being descends to earth through conception it dies as far as the spiritual world is concerned, leaving this corpse behind.

Just as the corpse of the physical human being is dissolved into earthly elements, so is the aspect of spirit and soul dissolved in the spiritual world, thus becoming the power which unfolds in physical thoughts. Our world of thoughts is the corpse of our spirit-and-soul aspect. Just as the earth makes use of the corpse when it is laid into the ground, or just as fire makes use of it when it is cremated, so in our physical world of thought do we make use throughout our life of our spirit-and-soul corpse.[30]

Sense of self and will—transformed fear

The second thing is what we have to call fear. This, too, is metamorphosed in such a way that it falls into two parts. The first, which is what we experience as fear before our descent into the earthly world, which entirely fills the soul and makes us want to flee from the spiritual world, becomes something different when we enter into our body; this initially expresses itself within the human being as something which I should like to call the sense of self. The sense of self is indeed fear that has been transformed. The fact that you feel yourself to be a self, the fact that you yourself are contained within yourself, this is metamorphosed fear from the life before birth.

The second part into which fear is transformed is will. Everything that comes to work as impulses of the will, everything on which our activity in the world is founded, is present as fear prior to our descent into earthly life . . .

When you look into yourself, the first thing you see is, though, your sense of self. This is something which should not be too much enhanced by means of education; otherwise one would be too much inclined towards megalomania when entering the spiritual world. But in the depths of your will impulses you will everywhere find that fear is lurking, and you must be strengthened against this fear.

So basically you will find in the exercises given in my book *How to Know Higher Worlds* that the aim is to endure the fear of which we become aware in the manner just described. This fear is something that must be present among the forces of development, otherwise the human being would not at all want to enter into earthly existence from out of the spiritual world. He would not flee away from the spiritual world. He would not develop the impulse to enter into the limitations of the physical human body. The fact that after living for a while between death and a new birth he does develop this inclination is connected with the fear of the spiritual world, which he feels as an entirely natural characteristic of his soul.[31]

A feeling of acceptance towards the future engenders fearlessness

But when on the other hand we approach the things of the external world they always appear to us to be mingled with what we might call 'the dark womb of the future', so those who look more closely will be obliged to say: 'In everything I approach within the external world there is always something of the future.' There is always something that repels us if we feel fear and anxiety about whatever might befall us. The external world stands there before us as though enveloped in a dense veil. But when we generate the feeling of acceptance and the mood of prayer towards what is coming to meet us out of the dark womb of the future we discover that we can face all the beings of the external world with the same assuredness and hope that comes to meet us out of the feeling of acceptance. Whatever we might be faced with, we can then say: 'The wisdom of the world will shine towards me!' Whereas otherwise nothing but gloom glares at us out of everything we meet, so that darkness enters our soul, we shall now see how the sense of acceptance in us causes the feeling to arise that fundamentally it can only be through the highest which we long for and desire in our soul that the wisdom-filled content of the world will shine towards us out of everything.

So now we can say: It is the hope of enlightenment from out of our entire environment that will come to us through the mood of acceptance achieved in prayer. Just as the darkness encloses us within ourselves, just as the darkness shows us forlornness and narrowness even in our physical surroundings when we find ourselves in the gloom of night where blackness spreads all around us, so do we feel, when morning comes and the light shines upon us, how we are taken and placed outside ourselves; not, however, in a way that makes us lose ourselves but as though we were able to carry into the outside world the best will of our soul as well as the most earnest aspiration of our soul. In this way we feel how a spreading-out into the world which alienates us from ourselves is overcome by the warmth of prayer which brings us back to ourselves. And when we can bring the warmth of prayer to unfold within us until it becomes the feeling of acceptance which can flow through prayer, then the warmth of prayer will ignite and become the light of prayer. Then we shall step out of ourselves anew, knowing: If we now unite ourselves with the external world and if we turn our gaze towards all that exists in the world around us, we shall not feel scattered about and estranged from ourselves; instead we shall feel how all that is best in our soul flows out of it so that we feel united with that which shines towards us out of the world around us.[32]

Fear of the future stunts our development

Those who look with anxiety and fear towards whatever the future may bring them hinder their development and stunt the free unfolding of their soul forces. Nothing is more obstructive for the free unfolding of soul forces than are fear and anxiety about the unknown which enter the soul out of the stream of the future.[33]

Composure over against what the future may hold

In its ideal form this state of composed resignation would consist of a soul mood that could continuously say to itself: 'Whatever is to come, whatever the next hour, the next morning might bring, since it is entirely unknown to me I cannot change it however fearful or anxious I may feel; so I shall await it with perfect inner peace of my soul, with perfect ocean stillness of my mind!' The experience that arises out of this feeling of composed resignation towards the future has the following consequence: an individual who can live towards the future with such resignation and with perfect ocean stillness of his mind, without forfeiting his energy in any way, will be able to unfold the forces of his soul most intensely, in the freest manner possible. It is as though one hindrance after another were to drop away from his soul, as though that mood were increasingly to come upon his soul which has been characterized as a 'feeling of acceptance' towards the events that flow towards us out of the future.

It is not possible for the soul to arrive at this feeling of composure by means of a peremptory command or an arbitrary whim. It is a feeling that results from something we might describe as the other mood of prayer, the mood of prayer which is directed towards the future and its wisdom-filled course of events. To submit to what we call the divine wisdom in events, ever and again to call up in oneself the thought and the feeling, indeed the impulse of the life of the mind that whatever will come will be as it must, and that in one direction or another it must produce its good effects, to bring about this mood in one's soul and to live within this mood in words, in feelings, in ideas—that is the second form of the mood of prayer, the mood of composure in prayer.[34]

A mood of prayer evokes trust in the future

Thus the mood of prayer leads us on the one hand to a consideration of our narrowly limited 'I' which has worked its way from the past up until the present and which, when we examine it, clearly shows us how infinitely more there is in us than we have utilized. And on the other hand this consideration leads us into the future, showing us how infinitely more there is that can flow into our 'I' out of the unknown womb of the future than this 'I' has yet grasped in the present time. Every mood of prayer must be brought into one of these two moods. If we can take hold of this mood of prayer and make the prayer into an expression of this mood, then shall we find in the prayer itself that force which leads us out beyond our narrow self. For what is prayer of this kind other than a shining forth of the force in us that strives to go beyond what our 'I' has been in a specific moment! And once the 'I' strives fully outwards, then the force which is the force of development is alive in it. If we can learn from the past that we have more within us than we have utilized, then our prayer is a cry to the divine world to come to us, to fill us with its presence! When we have reached this understanding in our feelings, then will prayer have become the source of onward development in us. So then we shall be able to count prayer among the forces of development within our 'I'.

And we can take the mood of prayer in a similar way with regard to the future if we are filled with fear and anxiety when faced with what the future might bring. For if that is the case we lack the composure which comes to us through prayer and which we send out towards our destinies that are hurrying towards us from out of the future and about which we have stated: The wisdom of the world has imposed them upon us. The effect of submitting to this mood of composure is different from sending out fear and anxiety towards what is approaching us. Our development is hampered by anxiety and fear. Through the waves of fear and anxiety we repel what is endeavouring to enter our soul from the future. But we approach it in fruitful hopefulness, allowing it to enter into us, if we turn the direction of our life towards it in composed resignation. So this composed resignation, which appears to diminish our stature, is in fact a strong force carrying us towards the future, so that the future can enrich the content of our soul and take our development to ever new stages.[35]

Openness

So we must learn to be without wishes in respect of future experiences; we must learn to become someone who has no wishes, and we must especially learn to break our habit of being afraid and anxious about future events. We must unrelentingly say to ourselves: 'I am prepared to accept anything that comes towards me, whatever it may be.' And we must express this not just as a dry and abstract idea but as our inmost feeling. There is no need to be fatalistic about this, for it is up to us to take a hand in our life. We are fatalists if we think that everything happens of its own accord. To inoculate our 'I' with this absolute equilibrium as a feeling is to bring a force to bear within our being of spirit and soul which can exclude the 'I' from perceptions which are already beginning to take up a position in our consciousness. In this way we shall remain within the world of the 'I' while also taking in a new world of soul experiences. These alone now enable us to see our inmost human core in its true, individual form which, although it has from birth been developing as that which stems from a previous life, has not as yet been truly recognized as such.[36]

Equanimity towards the future helps us to view former earth lives

If you really do this, if you learn above all to acquire a view into former lives by looking towards the future with equanimity and composure and without any wishes, you will discover that former lives on earth are not merely a logical conclusion but that on the basis of newly developed, genuine memories they will prove to be a reality. For this to come about, one thing is necessary. The ability to look into the past can only be acquired by remaining without wishes towards the future while also retaining equanimity and composure. In the degree to which we are prepared to experience the future in our feeling life and in the degree to which we shall be able to eliminate our 'I' with regard to experiencing the future, in that same degree shall we become capable of looking back into the past. The more we develop this equanimity the sooner will the time come when our past lives become a reality for us.[37]

4. COURAGE FOR EQUANIMITY— OVERCOMING FEAR

Face every event calmly and confidently

The first thing we must learn is to stand firm. This means that we must be securely anchored within the confusions of the life which surrounds us and that we no longer know any fear or anxiety but instead are able to regard every event, whatever it may be, with calmness and confidence.[38]

Apprehension obstructs access to the spiritual world

A specific disposition of soul is a prerequisite for the attainment of spiritual knowledge. This disposition of the soul is in some ways the opposite of the disposition needed for outer life on the physical plane. In outer life, especially in our present time, the soul is basically in a constant state of unrest. Hour after hour during the course of the day it receives ever-changing impressions and since it identifies totally with the impressions it receives this means that it is in a constant state of unrest.

Someone who wishes to press forward into the spiritual world will be obliged to achieve the opposite state. The very first condition that must be fulfilled for the ascent into the spiritual world is a state of complete peace, continuous inner peace in the soul. But it is more difficult to achieve this inner peace than one might imagine. We must hold our tongue in order to bring about this inner peace; and above all we have to forgo any excitement, all worries, all anxieties, even our normal interests in external life, for the duration of the period in which we intend to enter into the spiritual world. To enable matters of the spiritual world to pass before us we must be as though tied to a single location in the world while lacking any will to move away from it even by only a short distance. We have to remember that in everyday life on the physical plane we can move from one thing to another; the things are simply there. This is not the case in the spiritual world. In the spiritual world we have to use our thinking, our power of imagination, to fetch the things to where we are situated in the fixed location. We must as it were step outside ourselves and enter into the things before bringing them to ourselves from the outside. In doing this we have experiences which can be alarming for our soul.[39]

Courage in facing the terrors of higher worlds

The pupil seeking initiation will have to bring with him a kind of *courage* and *fearlessness* which he has developed in a specific way. He must purposefully seek out opportunities through which these virtues can be developed. They must be trained systematically during the course of esoteric schooling. Life as such is in itself a good esoteric school in this respect, indeed perhaps even the best. The esoteric pupil must want to remain calm in the face of danger and to tackle difficulties without any timid hesitation. When faced with danger he must, for example, immediately set about generating the feeling: 'My fear is absolutely useless in any direction; I must not entertain it at all; I must think solely about what is to be done.' And with regard to situations in which he has formerly been fearful he must reach the point at which 'being afraid' and 'losing courage' are impossibilities within his inner feelings. By educating himself in this way the pupil will develop certain quite specific powers which he will need if he is to be initiated into higher mysteries. Just as physically the human being needs the strength of his nerves in order to make use of his physical senses, so at the level of the soul does the pupil need the power which can only be developed by persons of a courageous and fearless disposition.

This is because someone who is pressing forward towards the higher mysteries will see things which illusions generated by the senses keep hidden from ordinary individuals. Although the physical senses prevent us from viewing higher truths they are, in this sense, also our benefactors. Through them things are hidden from us which would, if we were unprepared, plunge us into utter bewilderment, for we should be unable to bear the sight of them. But the esoteric pupil must be able to bear the sight of such things. He loses certain supports which in the outer world he owed to the fact of having been deceived. It is literally just as if one were to draw the attention of someone to a danger which had long been threatening him but of which he had been unaware. Although previously he was not afraid, now he is overcome by fear even though his new knowledge has in no way increased the danger.[40]

Being resigned in the face of failure

It is above all a matter of cultivating this courage and this fearlessness in the very depths of one's life of thought. The esoteric pupil must learn not to lose heart on account of a failure. He must be able to entertain the thought: 'I will forget that I have yet again failed in this matter; instead I will endeavour to try it once more as though nothing has happened.' This is how he can strive to reach the conviction that the sources of strength in the world on which he can draw are inexhaustible. He strives ever and again towards the spiritual which will lift and bear him regardless of how often his earthly aspect might have proved to be powerless and weak. He must be capable of striving towards the future in his life without permitting any experience from the past to hinder him.[41]

Overcoming inner fears

Most important of all in esoteric development is our endeavour to bear patiently all pain, suffering and fearfulness with inner firmness. This is the first important condition. It is not a good sign when an esoteric pupil complains all the time and tries out all kinds of cures for his ailments. Instead we have to realize that a change is taking place involving the members of our being and that this change will inevitably bring about conditions of anxiety and pain. All kinds of nervous conditions may also be noticed such as, for instance, claustrophobia and so on. All kinds of things can befall us. On the other hand we must realize very clearly that all these things are maya, illusion, and that these and similar manifestations will in reality give us strength in the face of other difficulties in our inner development which will occur later and also need to be overcome.

In all of this let us be guided by the thought that we are actually beloved of the gods the more we have to suffer and overcome! This will give us the kind of strength and firmness we shall need as we proceed along our path.

One of the first psychological difficulties to be encountered is loneliness of soul, a feeling of being non-existent as far as others are concerned. Yet it is this very loneliness that will vouchsafe us the highest spiritual benefits. Praying and meditating in solitude will bring us the highest and most powerful spiritual progression while also strengthening our individuality.[42]

An exercise for the development of equanimity

Make sure that no joy runs away with you, that no sorrow knocks you to the ground, that nothing goads you to excessive fury or anger, that no expectation fills you with anxiety or foreboding, that no situation leaves you nonplussed and so on. Do not fear that an exercise like this will make you dull or unable to enjoy life. On the contrary, you will soon notice that in the part of your soul where this exercise is taking place more refined characteristics will appear. Above all you will, with your more subtle attentiveness, one day begin to perceive an inner calmness in your body. Allow this to pour ... into your whole body by letting it flow from your heart towards your hands and feet and finally into your head. This can of course not occur after doing the exercise only once, for we are concerned here not with a single exercise but with a continuous attentiveness towards one's inner life of soul. You will have to call up this inner calmness at least once a day and then carry out the exercise of letting it stream out from the heart.[43]

A greater capacity for knowledge through combating fearfulness

Among the traits which we should struggle to control, such as vexation and anger, we must also count fearfulness, superstition and prejudice, vanity and ambition, inquisitiveness and the compulsion to provide unnecessary information, judging others according to social standing, gender or nationality, and so on. In this day and age it will be quite difficult to understand how battling against such traits can have anything to do with increasing one's capacity for higher knowledge. Nevertheless, every student of the esoteric will know that much more depends on such things than on a broadening of one's intelligence or on practising artistic skills. Misunderstandings can arise in particular if one believes that being fearless involves being foolhardy or that battling against prejudice concerning a person's social standing, race and so on means that one must disregard the differences that exist among human beings. In fact we only learn to recognize higher knowledge properly when we are no longer imprisoned in our prejudices. Even in the ordinary way of things it is right to recognize that fear of something prevents me from assessing it clearly, and that racial prejudice prevents me from looking into the soul of another human being. The esoteric pupil must develop this ordinary sense in himself in great subtlety and acuteness.[44]

Looking the spirit in the eye without fear or hope

Does the human spirit live before birth and after death, and what is the destiny of mankind in time and in eternity? Naturally most people approach these questions not without interest. And it is only natural that all the personal interest we can muster and all that we might experience by way of hope and fear—those two feelings which forever accompany us—must be closely bound up with questions pertaining to the eternal life of the spirit. In ancient times and places the establishments where the loftiest questions concerning the life of the spirit were taught and explained to pupils were called mystery schools. Pupils at those mystery schools were not taught in an abstract way about such matters. The truths were not handed down to them until their soul and spirit, indeed their whole personality, had developed a disposition that enabled them to see the subject matter in the right light. This disposition meant that the pupils had to have moved beyond joy and sorrow and above all beyond fear and hope, those two feelings with which people are so much tied up day after day and hour after hour. It was necessary to begin by removing these feelings from the personality. The pupils had to be purged of fear and hope. A purging was the preparation that the pupils had to undergo. Without this their questions remained unanswered. To be purged of the passions of joy and sorrow, of fear and hope, this was the precondition for climbing up to the summit of the mountain upon which the question of immortality could be discussed. It was clear that in this condition the pupil could look the spirit in the eye in the same way as a person can in spirit look a mathematical problem, purely objective mathematics, in the eye without passion, without being harassed by fear or hope.[45]

Selflessness overcomes fear

The esoteric pupil must say to himself over and over again that he will be unable to participate in the spiritual world until he has learnt to tell himself: 'I am full of egoism—and I can be no different so long as I find myself here on the physical plane; nevertheless, whatever part of me there is that lives here on the physical plane is only an image of me, a model which is a picture of my archetype. This model, this picture is utterly steeped in egoism. And it is universal karma which steeps us entirely in egoism as we pass along our path of development from incarnation to incarnation. World karma, however, is God. God also lives in us. And if we succeed in acting with goodness and nobility, it is the God in us who urges us on. And the God in us who urges us to act with goodness and nobility lives within our archetypal image. I myself am filled with egoism—but I am predetermined to become an image of my divine archetype. This archetype once resided in the midst of the Godhead— but it has descended into this physical form, and this physical form resides under the power of the God who stands above my destiny and my karma; and it is this physical form which is entirely steeped in egoism. Never, but never may I maintain that I am without egoism, for that can never be true—it is impossible for me to reside on the physical plane without egoism.

But if I learn how to look upon my archetype which is born of God, and if I permit my thinking, my feeling and my will, all the power of my soul to die utterly into this archetype, then I may be permitted to hope that I shall conquer the egoism within me and thus come closer to my archetype. We shall notice that as we grow more selfless we become physically stronger in the same measure. We shall notice that we no longer feel fear or alarm and that we no longer flinch when something startles us. We shall grow mighty and strong in the whole being of our humanity.[46]

The transformation of fear into reverence

All that we have within us by way of lusts, urges and passions billows and surges within our sentient soul. But as human beings we also needed a counterbalance for our egoism. This was understood by the former guiding powers of human evolution, and so they also laid fear into our sentient soul. Notice is drawn to this in the Mystery Drama *The Guardian of the Threshold.* It was essential for the human being to have fear because he would otherwise have seized everything for himself; and as a result his egoism would have grown too strong. Teachers in olden times were also clearly aware of this, and one of the features among the education methods they propounded was the telling of fairy tales and ghost stories. In modern education the telling of ghost stories to children is entirely lacking. Yet to a certain degree it is necessary for children's souls to hear such stories, namely to the extent that they call forth *wonderment* in the soul, which in turn evolves into reverence for something unknown. A child who has never been told of something unknown or sublime will never be able to feel reverence in later life.

The esoteric pupil must consciously transform fear into reverence, piety, devotion and the willingness to make sacrifices. When one enters the spiritual world fear must be transformed into reverence. That is why it is good to cultivate this on the physical plane. But if the feeling of fear is exaggerated in the human being, and if the 'I' is not strong enough to prevent not only the soul but also the physical body from being seized by it, then, for example, what we know as raving madness can set in. This can always be traced back to a weakness of the 'I' . . .

In our physical existence we ought to bear with equanimity whatever our destiny imposes upon us while also cultivating the feeling that none of all this has anything to do with us; we should accept it all with calmness and composure as though even our body were a stranger to us. Similarly we should arouse the feeling in ourselves not that it is we who have been chosen to make progress but that it is equally delightful when others also make as much progress as we do. As far as the evolution of the world is concerned it is all the same whoever it is who makes progress. But for ourselves the essential factor is our battle for the transformation of egoism.[47]

An exercise for doing away with fear

In the morning, decide to carry out an action at a specific time in the afternoon; think this through in every detail. Do this exercise for four to eight weeks.

Another exercise requires you to decide on an action on the first day, to think it through on the fourth day and to carry it out on the seventh day.

And here is another exercise:

On day 1: Decision and preparation of all the physical requirements—character traits
On day 12: Vivid inner pictures, thinking through with love, imaginative
On day 19: Think over your own strengths and capabilities
On day 23: View the hindrances
On day 27: Prepare with love
On day 30: Carry out the exercise[48]

Not being afraid of fear

Having reached a certain stage in his development, the spiritual researcher will realize: 'In the world which I am endeavouring to enter I can no longer cling to the firm support of external sense perceptions, and neither can I be supported by the kind of judgements which I have trained myself to hold with my intellect.' This is a significant and serious moment in the life of the spiritual researcher, for now he feels as though firm ground is slipping away from him, as though he has lost the support which he had in ordinary life, as though all safety is gone, as though he is approaching an abyss into which he must fall with every further step. This is an experience to which every kind of spiritual schooling has to lead. However, all true spiritual schooling of the present day makes sure that it is an experience which is not bound up with all manner of danger ...

In a schooling of this kind the fear and anxiety of ordinary life are just as much reinforced and augmented as are selfishness and egoism. They grow into something that is like a force of nature. And here something must be said which might sound like a paradox. In ordinary life, if we have not developed some degree of courage in ourselves, if we are cowards in some way, we can be startled by one event or another. But if we are not cowards we can withstand our shock. In the realm of the soul we have been describing, fear and shock and horror may approach us, but we must be capable of not being afraid of the fear and not being startled by the shock, of not being anxious about the anxiety. This is the paradox, but it is definitely a genuine soul experience in this realm.[49]

Surviving fearlessly in an increasingly inimical external world

During the course of human evolution the external world around us grows continuously more inimical. More and more you will have to learn to oppose the encroaching external world with your inner strength. But fear must be made to disappear while you do this. Most especially for those who undergo an esoteric training it is necessary, indeed unavoidably necessary, that they should free themselves of all feelings of fear and anxiety. There is some justification for fear only when it draws our attention to the need to be strong; but all unnatural feelings of fear that torment us must be made to disappear entirely. What is supposed to happen when someone still has feelings of anxiety and fear at the moment when the Jupiter* consciousness begins? On Jupiter human beings will be faced with an external world that is far, far more inimical and terrible than that of today. Those who fail to rid themselves of fear while they are on the earth will tumble from one terrifying horror to another.

Even now this situation is increasingly being prepared in the external world ... Today's culture is itself creating the horrible monsters which will threaten human beings on Jupiter. Look at the gigantic machines being constructed with every ingenuity by means of human technology! In such machines we are creating the demons that will rage against us in the future. Whatever technical apparatuses and machines human beings build today will in future come to life and torment us in terrible ways. All the things that serve only

---

* Steiner's term for a future incarnation of the Earth. (Ed.)

utilitarian purposes or which are created out of individual or overall egoism will be our enemies in the future.

Nowadays we are much too much concerned with the usefulness of what we do. If we truly want to promote development we should not ask whether something is useful but whether it is beautiful or noble. We should not act purely in accordance with utilitarian principles, but instead out of pure enjoyment of what is beautiful. All the things that human beings create today in order to satisfy their artistic needs and out of pure love for what is beautiful, all these things will also come to life in the future and will contribute to the advancement of human development.

Today it is terrible to see how many thousands of people are encouraged from their earliest childhood to carry out activities that serve only materialistic purposes while all their lives they remain cut off from anything beautiful or artistic. The most marvellous works of art ought to be displayed even in the poorest primary schools. This would generate endless blessings for human development.

We human beings are building our own future. We can gain an idea of what things will be like on Jupiter when we realize that today nothing exists which is entirely good or entirely evil. Good and evil are intermingled in every individual today. Those who are good must always say to themselves that they have only a little more good than evil in themselves, not that as such they are entirely good. On Jupiter, however, good and evil will no longer be mixed together; there human beings will be divided into those who are entirely good and those who are entirely evil. Whatever we cultivate today by way of the good and the noble will serve to strengthen the good on Jupiter while all things created only from the viewpoint of egoism or utility will there strengthen the evil.[50]

The power of spiritual thoughts

The teachings of spiritual science amount to a collection of ideas that lead us into supersensible worlds, so when we think about spiritual science it is necessary for us to raise ourselves towards higher realms. For every lesson in spiritual science the soul has to reach up beyond everyday life. As soon as we turn towards the teachings we remove ourselves into another world with our thinking. Our 'I' then unites with the spiritual world, and if we consider that it is out of this spiritual world that our 'I' is born we realize that in thinking about spiritual science we are entering with our 'I' into our spiritual home, the original source from which it stems.

If we understand this rightly we must, in truth, compare spiritual-scientific thinking with something which—from a spiritual point of view—we recognize as the state of sleep. When the human being goes to sleep in the evening and thus enters into the spiritual world, he finds himself in the very world out of which his 'I' has been born and from which he departs again every morning in order to return to the world of the senses within his physical body. One day the soul will live consciously within this spiritual world; but in normal human consciousness the 'I' is not consciously within it ...

Spiritual-scientific thinking gives us the strength gradually to make a conscious connection with these spiritual worlds. Because anthroposophy takes us into those worlds at least in our thinking, it has some characteristics—beneficial characteristics—in common with sleep. In sleep all the cares and afflictions arising out of the world of the senses cease. If we can sleep so that our thinking is extinguished we forget all our worries. This is the most beneficial effect of sleeping and it derives from the fact that during sleep the 'I' opens itself to the currents of the spiritual world which then flow into it. The currents have strengthening powers and because of these not only are the cares and afflictions forgotten during sleep but in addition the damage done to our organism by those cares and afflictions is overcome. Whatever has made them troubling is extinguished by the spiritual powers, hence the refreshment and rebirth which all healthy sleep vouchsafes us. These are the characteristics which spiritual-scientific thinking has in common with sleep in the higher sense.

Spiritual thoughts are powerful thoughts if we grasp them in a living way. If we raise ourselves up to thoughts about the past and the future of the earth and allow these magnificent happenings to work on us, then our soul will be drawn to them in fascination and transported far away. When we think about how the ideal of our own sovereign will-power arises out of the karmic plan of our destiny, such thoughts give us the courage and strength to say: 'Even if today one obstacle or another in my life remains insurmountable, nevertheless my strength will grow from one incarnation to the next. My sovereign will is going to grow ever stronger within me, and all the obstacles I meet will help me make this will more sovereign still. I shall overcome the obstacles and on account of this my will-power is going to develop more and more as also will my energy. The trivialities of life, all that is paltry in my existence, will melt away like hoar frost in the sun, that sun which rises in the wisdom which fills us when we think spiritually. The world of our feelings will be filled with warmth, with glowing heat and shining light; our existence will expand and we shall experience the bliss of being within it.'

If we repeat such moments and let their effect work on us, the consequence will be a strengthening of our whole existence in every direction. Although it will not happen from one day to the next, constant repetition of such thoughts will cause our gloom, our constant dissatisfaction with our lot, our grumbling temperament to disappear little by little. Knowledge and recognition of the spirit will become a healing medicine for our soul! And when this happens, when our existence expands in this way, this medicine will plant the fruits of spiritual knowledge in our soul. What comes about within us on account of this will be the ideal of spiritual science. All the strife and discord of life will fall when confronted with the harmonious thoughts and feelings that arise as a consequence of an energetic will. Spiritual science will thereby prove to be not only a knowledge and a teaching but also a force for life and content for our soul. And when it is understood in this way it will become capable of working in life in a way that will lift all cares and worries from the shoulders of human beings.[51]

Ridding oneself of worries
Through our physical body we are embedded in the physical world. The more we feel bound up in this world the more do we cut ourselves off from the spirit. We should not become immersed in worries. Of course we must in every way do our

duty, we must do what is necessary even if others disapprove; but we must not sink into despondency, we must not 'die into matter'. It is very difficult to achieve a proper balance with regard to how much trouble we should take, how much we should 'worry' about our daily life and how and when we should rise above this. In all this we can only do the right thing if we recognize the Christ-principle. If we permit Christ to be born in us, if we do not 'die into matter' but into Christ, then we shall have grasped what is right, what is good and what is true. In this way we have an effect on the physical . . .

There is a kind of substantiality in which our worries live, and there are highly developed individuals who take this substantiality of worries into themselves. In esoteric language they are termed 'men of sorrows'. The greatest 'Man of Sorrows' was Christ, and it is not without reason that we may read: 'Cast all your sorrows upon him.'

If we understand these words correctly, we must know that we have to pass all our sorrows beyond a certain level on to Christ in their substantiality so that we may continue to press forward in the right way.[52]

Courage surrounds us on all sides

You see, the knowledge you gain with regard to a medicament—if it is truly an imaginative or inspired knowledge, then the medicament will possess healing forces; and this need not even be your own imagination, it can be that of someone else, as I have often said. The idea you have for what might be a medicament is effective, but it is only effective so long as you are without fear. Fear is the opposite of love. If you enter a sickroom with fear, whatever therapy you administer will be ineffective. But if you enter the sickroom with love, without thought of yourself, if you can direct your whole soul to those you are going to heal, if you can live in the love of your imaginative, inspired knowledge, then you will enter into the process of healing not as someone whose knowledge is born out of fear but as someone whose knowledge is born out of love. In this way medicine is taken into the moral realm not only from the outside but also from within.

So in the realm of medicine—as in all realms where spiritual knowledge is applied—there is a strong need to develop courage. You know that we are surrounded on all sides by courage. The air is an illusion; it is courage that surrounds us on all sides. If we wish to live in the world where we breathe, it is courage that we need. If we are cowards, in whatever way, we do not live within the world for we exclude ourselves; we only appear to breathe. What you need more than anything else if you want to study medicine is courage, the courage to heal. It is a fact that if you approach an illness with the courage to heal, then you have the correct orientation which in 90 per cent of cases will lead to the desired result.[53]

Inner fearlessness as a prerequisite for holding one's own in the supersensible world

So the soul reaches the point at which it feels itself to be in opposition to the supersensible world, and therefore it has to tell itself: 'I am not fit to become one with that world, yet it is only that world which can show me true reality and at the same time also how I am relating to true reality; I have separated myself off from proper observation of what is true.' This feeling signifies an experience that will increasingly be decisive for the whole value of our own soul. We feel that with the whole of our life we are steeped in an error. Yet this error differs from other errors. They are thinking errors, whereas this is an error of experience. An error in thinking is removed when we replace the incorrect thought with the correct one. But an error that is experienced is a part of our whole soul make-up. We *are* the error. We cannot simply correct it, for whatever we may think, it exists, it is a part of reality, a part of our very own reality. An experience like this is destructive for our very self. We feel our inner being to be painfully repelled by everything for which we long.

When such pain is felt at a stage of our soul journey it exceeds any pain it is possible to feel in the world of the senses. And for this reason it can surpass whatever else we have thus far coped with on our journey. There can be something numbing about it. Our soul is faced with the alarming question: 'Where shall I find the strength with which to bear the burden laid upon me?' It has to find this strength within its own life. This strength consists of something we might call inner courage, inner fearlessness.

In order to proceed on the journey of our soul we must be led to the realization that it is from our inner being that the powers can come which give us inner courage and inner fearlessness such as are not needed for life in the body we possess in the sense-perceptible world. Such powers can only arise out of true self-knowledge. Indeed it is only at this stage of development that we begin to realize how little we have hitherto known about our self. We have simply given ourselves over to inner experiences instead of observing them as one would observe a part of the external world. However, through the steps that have led to the capacity to have experiences outside the body we receive special means for the acquisition of self-knowledge. We learn how to observe ourselves from a point of view that only arises when we are outside the physical body ...

It is in the nature of the human soul for us to feel pain when faced with such revelations about ourselves. When we experience this pain we come to realize how strong the obvious longing is to regard ourselves, just as we are, as valuable and important human beings. It may seem an ugly fact that this is so. But we must freely come to terms with this ugliness of our own self. Previously we have not noticed this ugliness for the simple reason that we have hitherto never properly entered into our own being with consciousness. Only now do we notice how we love those things in our self which we should now feel to be something ugly. The might of self-love reveals itself in all its immensity ...

We look back towards our whole soul and towards our 'I' as something that we must now lay aside if we want to enter into the supersensible world. But before entering the supersensible world the soul cannot help regarding this 'I' as its true being. It is compelled to regard it as its true human being. It has to say to itself: 'Through this "I" of mine I must develop ideas about the world; if I do not want to regard myself as a lost being I must not lose this "I" of mine.' The strongest urge in the soul is everywhere to preserve the 'I' for itself so as not to lose entirely the ground beneath its feet. What the soul feels to be completely justified in ordinary life

it is not permitted to feel as it enters supersensible surroundings. It has to cross a threshold where it has to leave
something behind; and this is not merely some possession or
other which it feels to be valuable, but that which until this
moment it has considered to be its very self. It must be
capable of saying to itself: 'What thus far has been valid as my
strongest truth I must now, beyond the threshold to the
supersensible world, be able to see as my strongest error.'

The soul may well shy away from such a demand. It may so
strongly feel that what it ought to be doing is a kind of giving
up on itself, a declaration that its own being is a nothingness,
that having arrived at the threshold it more or less confesses
to itself that it is powerless to carry out what is required of
it...

What ought to happen upon entering into the supersensible world is that we make ourselves capable of laying
aside whatever it is we feel to be the strongest truth in
ordinary life and set about a different way of feeling and
judging things. We have to realize, though, that when we then
return to the world of sense perceptions we once again have
to have feelings and make judgements that are appropriate
for this world. We have to learn not only to live in two worlds
but to live in a completely different way in each of these. We
must not spoil our ability to make proper judgements in the
ordinary world of senses and intellect on account of being
obliged to use a different way of making judgements in
another world.

It is difficult for a human being to adopt this position, and
we can only gain the ability to do so by means of continuous
energetic and patient work on strengthening our life of soul.

When we undergo the experiences which await us at the threshold we will feel how beneficial it is that one is not led up to the threshold in one's ordinary life of soul. We will sense that this blessing stems from a spiritual entity who at the threshold protects the human being against the danger of experiencing the shocks of self-destruction.

A different world lies behind the external world of our daily life. A stern guardian stands at the threshold to that supersensible world and he it is who ensures that we do not know anything about its laws. All the doubts and uncertainties about that world are, after all, easier to bear than the sight of what we must leave behind when we want to enter it.

We remain protected against the experiences described so long as we do not approach this threshold of our own accord. Even if others describe to us the experiences they have had when approaching or crossing this threshold this does not change the fact that we are protected. Indeed, it can be a help to us when we approach the threshold ourselves if we have been given such descriptions. In this case, as in many others, we can accomplish something better if we have prior ideas about it. However, knowing about such things in advance has no bearing on what the wanderer in the supersensible world has to learn by way of self-knowledge.[54]

Hypochondria and the helper syndrome

If there were only love in the world nothing would exist there; the opposite force must always restore the balance. Today, therefore, we shall be pointing out forces and beings which work within us bringing about those peculiar conditions that are familiar to every esoteric pupil.

The first condition is that of a bad mood, a mood which seems to come about for no particular reason and which can be set off by any trifling detail before growing in intensity to such an extent that the nature of the person in question appears to be entirely transformed. In this case we are dealing with beings from the hierarchy of the Primal Creative Forces who are bringers of healing if they remain within their own domain but who cause damage if they trespass out of their own region and into that of the Spirits of Form. They are called Spirits of Weight and it is they who help us when we wake up from sleep by drawing us down to the level of the earth. This is why we so often have a sensation of heaviness, of inertia when we wake up. But if we add the bad mood to this, these spirits then work to our disadvantage and make everything heavy and dark for us. They influence the physical body and fill it with heaviness so that we feel fettered to the earth. If our 'I' does not counteract this and does not sense the danger threatening it, then these spirits dominate the 'I'. We become powerless and sink into hypochondria. We all know how difficult it is to cure hypochondria. This illness always points to an effect from a former life as an esoteric researcher, for it cannot come about within a single life. Once the Spirits of Weight have taken hold of us in this way, this shows in diseases of the lower abdomen and the digestive organs.

We turn now to the Spirits of Light who also work in a healthy manner so long as they remain in their own sphere but who cause harm to human beings if they step outside their own domain and enter the realm of the Spirits of Movement. This is the case when a person imagines he must help the whole of mankind and wants to flow out entirely into loving kindness whereas what he actually craves is to rise higher in his development without making any effort. Then the Spirits of Light arrive, entering into this person and engendering visionary enthusiasm in him so that all his mental images become depictions of untruths. Such a person imagines himself to be a force for the good whose mission it is to improve the world. When we fall under the dominion of these spirits, the 'I' becomes utterly full of itself so that it can no longer interpret things that are outside it in the right way. And finally the person succumbs to a condition which affects his physical body by destroying the brain. However, if this person reacts against these forces and tries to grasp the fact that he is imagining things when he believes he can help everyone and so on, and if instead he endeavours to turn his forces away from those actions which seem to be founded on love, and if he endeavours to suppress his great urge to make spiritual progress and instead believes that the right maturity will appear at the right time, then these spirits will work as a healing force and bring him closer to the light step by step. These are the spirits who help bring us to the light in the evening when we go to sleep.

We must always be on our guard against these two forces; and if they make an appearance in our feelings we should immediately be on the alert and pay attention to what we ourselves are up to. If we are in a bad mood but have always been aware of it and fought against it, then a moment will come when our body feels utterly exhausted and aches all over. This will be the proof that we have won the battle. And if we tend towards visionary enthusiasm as described here, but have fought valiantly against it, then we shall begin to feel that we no longer have any legs to stand on and that our body is too light to be held down by the earth. And this will be the proof that we have won the battle with the Spirits of Light.

These are the consequences of the exercises when they are carried out in the right way. Instead of making us anxious or in a bad mood they should encourage us to move bravely forward. Having gradually learnt to understand that we are always surrounded by forces which work upon us we shall have come to understand how to live through the day in the fullness of our consciousness of self in such a way that we create a balance between all these influences.[55]

NOTES

Given that this volume is made up of quotations from Rudolf Steiner's works, Steiner's words have been translated afresh from the latest and most accurate German editions in order to keep a consistent flow to the language, tone and terminology. 'GA' stands for *Gesamtausgabe* or Collected Works of Rudolf Steiner in the original German. Complete volumes translated into English are shown in 'Sources' on page 70.

1. Fear and its Effects
1. GA 12.
2. Lecture in Berlin, 10 October 1907, GA 56.
3. Lecture in Berlin, 12 December 1907, GA 56.
4. Esoteric Lesson in Kassel, 26 February 1909, GA 266/1.
5. Lecture in Berlin, 12 December 1907, GA 56.
6. Lecture in Dornach, 23 September 1921, GA 207.
7. Esoteric Lesson in Berlin, 26 January 1908, GA 266/1.
8. Lecture in Berlin, 6 March 1913, GA 62.
9. Ibid.
10. Lecture in Berlin, 26 February 1916, GA 65.
11. Esoteric Lesson in Düsseldorf, 15 April 1909, GA 264.
12. Lecture in Berlin, 21 October 1907 (afternoon), GA 101.
13. Lecture in Dornach, 3 January 1919, GA 188.
14. Lecture in Stuttgart, 9 October 1922, GA 218.
15. Lecture in Berlin, 12 March 1909, GA 57.
16. Lecture in Berlin, 10 October 1907, GA 56.

2. Death, Fear of Death and Fear of the Unknown
17. Lecture in Munich, 24 August 1909, GA 113.
18. Ibid.
19. Lecture in Munich, 27 August 1911, GA 129.

20. Lecture in Dornach, 27 December 1918, GA 187.

21. Note, undated, GA 40.

22. Lecture in Berlin, 19 October 1911, GA 61.

23. Lecture in Kristiania (Oslo), 18 May 1923, GA 226.

24. Lecture in Berlin, 3 March 1910, GA 59.

25. Lecture in Berlin, 12 December 1907, GA 56.

26. Lecture in London, 2 May 1913, GA 152.

3. Fear of the Future and Trust in Destiny

27. Lecture in Bremen, 27 November 1910, *Beiträge zur Rudolf Steiner-Gesamtausgabe*, Booklet 98.

28. Lecture in Leipzig, 5 November 1911, GA 130.

29. Lecture in Heidenheim, 12 June 1919, GA 193.

30. Lecture in Dornach, 17 February 1922, GA 210.

31. Ibid.

32. Lecture in Berlin, 17 February 1910, GA 59.

33. Ibid.

34. Ibid.

35. Ibid.

36. Lecture in Berlin, 27 October 1910, GA 60.

37. Ibid.

4. Courage for Equanimity—Overcoming Fear

38. Esoteric Lesson in Berlin, 9 July 1904, GA 266/1.

39. Lecture in Milan, 26 October 1912, GA 140.

40. GA 10.

41. Ibid.

42. Esoteric Lesson in Karlsruhe, 14 October 1911, GA 266/2.

43. GA 267.

44. GA 10.

45. Lecture in Berlin, 30 March 1904, GA 52.

46. Esoteric Lesson in Berlin, 5 November 1910, GA 266/2.

47. Esoteric Lesson in Basel, 22 September 1912, GA 266/2.

48. Esoteric Lesson in Berlin, 9 October 1907, GA 266/1.

49. Lecture in Berlin, 6 March 1913, GA 62.

50. Esoteric Lesson in Munich, 16 January 1908, GA 266/1.

51. Lecture in Berlin, 25 May 1909, GA 109.

52. Esoteric Lesson in Kassel, 27 June 1909, GA 266/1.

53. Lecture in Dornach, 8 January 1924, GA 316.

54. GA 16.

55. Esoteric Lesson in Hamburg, 25 May 1910, GA 266/2.

SOURCES

The following volumes are cited in this book. Where relevant, published editions of equivalent English translations are given below the German titles.

The works of Rudolf Steiner are listed here (in brackets the latest edition) with the volume numbers of the complete works in German, the *Gesamtausgabe* (GA), as published by Rudolf Steiner Verlag, Dornach, Switzerland.

RSP = Rudolf Steiner Press, UK
AP/SB = Anthroposophic Press/SteinerBooks, USA

10   *Wie erlangt man Erkenntnisse der höheren Welten?* (1993)
      Knowledge of the Higher Worlds (RSP)
      How to Know Higher Worlds (SB)

12   *Stufen der höheren Erkenntnis* (1993)
      Stages of Higher Knowledge (AP)

16   *Ein Weg zur Selbsterkenntnis des Menschen* (2004)
      A Road to Self Knowledge and The Threshold of the Spiritual World (RSP)

40   *Wahrspruchworte* (2005)

52   *Spirituelle Seelenlehre und Weltbetrachtung* (1986)
      Spiritualism, Madame Blavatsky and Theosophy (SB)

56   *Die Erkenntnis der Seele und des Geistes* (1985)

57   *Wo und wie findet man den Geist?* (1984)

59   *Metamorphosen des Seelenlebens—Pfade der Seelenerlebnisse. Zweiter Teil* (1984)

60   *Antworten der Geisteswissenschaft auf die grossen Fragen des Daseins* (1983)
      Transforming the Soul, Vol. 2 (RSP)

61   *Menschengeschichte im Lichte der Geistesforschung* (1983)

62   *Ergebnisse der Geistesforschung* (1988)

266/1   *Aus den Inhalten der esoterischen Stunden. Gedächtnisaufzeichnungen von Teilnehmern. Band I: 1904–1909* (2007)
         Esoteric Lessons 1904–1909 (SB)

266/2   *Aus den Inhalten der esoterischen Stunden. Gedächtnisaufzeichnungen von Teilnehmern. Band II: 1910–1912* (1996)

267   *Seelenübungen Band I. Übungen mit Wort- und Sinnbild-Meditationen zur methodischen Entwicklung höherer Erkenntniskräfte, 1904–1924* (2001)

316   *Meditative Betrachtungen und Anleitungen zur Vertiefung der Heilkunst* (2008)
         Course for Young Doctors (Mercury Press)

All English-Language titles are available via Rudolf Steiner Press, UK (www.rudolfsteinerpress.com) or SteinerBooks, USA (www.steinerbooks.org)